Jazz Up Your Journal Writing

Grades 1–2

by
Dr. Phyllis J. Perry

Carson-Dellosa Publishing Company, Inc.
Greensboro, North Carolina

Credits

Editor:
Amy Gamble

**Layout Design
and Art Coordination:**
Jon Nawrocik

Inside Illustrations:
Stefano Giorgi

Cover Design:
Peggy Jackson

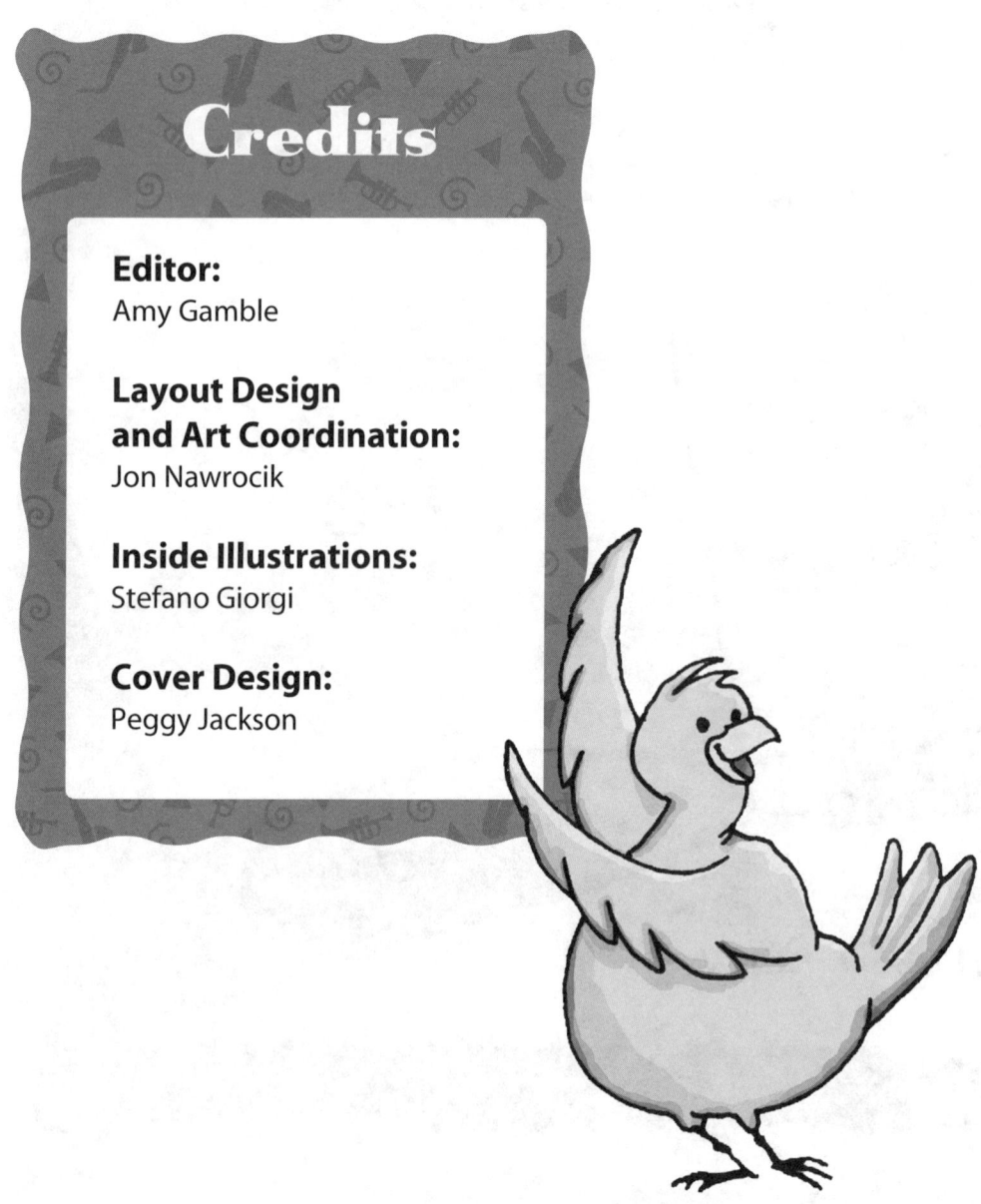

© 2003 Carson-Dellosa Publishing Company, Inc., Greensboro, North Carolina 27425. The purchase of this material entitles the buyer to reproduce worksheets and activities for classroom use only—not for commercial resale. Reproduction of these materials for an entire school or district is prohibited. No part of this book may be reproduced (except as noted above), stored in a retrieval system, or transmitted in any form or by any means (mechanically, electronically, recording, etc.) without the prior written consent of Carson-Dellosa Publishing Co., Inc.

Printed in the USA • All rights reserved.

ISBN 0-88724-193-X

Table of Contents

Introduction 4
Tips and Extensions 6

Language Arts
Alphabet Books 8
Animal Adjectives 9
Poetic Recipes 10
Happy Birthday! 11
Expressions 12
Interview with a Friend 13
Keys to Writing 14
Seasonal Sentences 15
Teddy Bear Adventures 16
Wordless Picture Book 17

Mathematics
Button, Button 18
Shapes All Around 19
Measuring Problem 20
One Half of a Whole 21
Animals from Space 22
Math Vocabulary 23
Math in Action 24
Roadside Stand 25
Number Poems 26
Saving for Goldfish 27

Science
Flowers 28
Sounds Around 29
Pet Particulars 30
Sight, Smell, and Touch 31
Living and Nonliving 32
Animal Features 33
Balanced Meal 34
Weather Watch 35
Weather Poems 36
Mystery Box 37

Social Studies
Community Helpers 38
What Do You Want? 39
Farm Life and City Life 40
Map It! 41
Where Am I? 42
Travel through Time 43
Folktales 44
Jobs in Your School 45
School Rules 46
Time to Celebrate! 47

Programmable Journal Page 48

Introduction

What is the purpose of journals in the classroom?

Journals can be one of several tools used to evaluate student learning. Journal entries can provide regular information, not only about the quality of a student's writing, but also about a student's thoughts and understanding in various subject areas. Journal writing that follows prompts like those included in this book can be exciting and satisfying to students and can serve as a valuable curricular tool.

Students need to understand that classroom journals are not private diaries. They should be aware from the beginning exactly how the journals will be used and who will be reading them. You may choose to read and comment on your students' journal entries. Or, journal entries might be shared with the class or a small group or lead to an oral discussion on a topic of interest.

How should journals be incorporated into class time?

Journal writing is most effective if it appears as a regular activity throughout the school week. You may select a time each day or two or three times a week for students to write in their journals. The length of writing sessions may vary, although 15 or 20 minutes seems to work well for elementary grade students. The period right after lunch is especially popular because it serves as a time for students to be quiet and settle down.

Sometimes journal writing might be unstructured. During these times, students may be invited to write whatever they wish, including their thoughts and feelings. But, often it is more useful if the journal writing is structured with a specific assignment. The assignment might be selected from this book, or it may be one that you originate that is centered around a particular subject, season, holiday, or current event.

How should journal entries be graded?

The decision to read and grade student journals is left to your discretion. Often, students will write more freely and enjoy journal writing more with the knowledge that their work will not be read or judged. However, if the journal is to be used for assessment purposes, at least reading and possibly grading would be necessary. Just be sure to let students know what the parameters are up front.

You should also consider the time involved in reading each student's journal. When only one or a few children are involved in a home-schooling situation, journal reading can easily be accomplished. In a school setting, it is advisable to read through about one-fifth of the classroom journals at a time. This way, the task does not become overwhelming.

Introduction

In order to give students practice in writing to communicate and to express their ideas and emotions, you may want to allow students to write freely without worrying about spelling. Correct spelling and vocabulary building can be addressed by having students keep personal dictionaries to which they can refer during journal writing time. You may also display a word wall or word lists related to topics being studied.

How should students' journals be made and organized?

To complete the activities in this book, each student needs a personal journal. The pages in this book are reproducible with space for students to write (including the backs of copied pages). It is recommended that each student use a three-ring binder as a journal. Then, pages can be copied and added as they are assigned, or all of the pages can be placed in the journals at the beginning of the year and completed as assigned. Photos or student artwork can be used to decorate the covers.

For ease of reading and grading journals, each student can add two blank pages to the beginning of his or her journal to use as a table of contents. Students can number their journal pages in the upper right hand corners; give titles to their stories, articles, and poems (or use the titles from the prepared prompts); and list these titles and page numbers in their tables of contents.

Several copies of the blank, programmable journal page (page 48) can be added to the end of each student's journal for unstructured writing. Or, you can use this page to write your own prompts and make copies for each student. You may also give individual students the opportunity to write journal prompts for the class.

About this book:

Jazz Up Your Journal Writing is full of suggestions to help teachers and home-schooling parents incorporate student journal writing into all four areas of the core curriculum—language arts, math, science, and social studies. The activities also address writing in both poetry and prose forms. Some pages offer literature suggestions for students to read that serve to introduce, extend, and enhance the lessons. Have these and/or other relevant books checked out from the library and available to students in the classroom as they complete the activities.

Most of the journal activities can be completed without additional materials or instruction. Any additional preparation or information needed is noted in the *Tips and Extensions* section (pages 6–7). Extensions for more in-depth writing or project ideas for activities are also included in this section.

Tips and Extensions

Alphabet Books (page 8): Provide a selection of alphabet books, like those suggested on the journal page, for students to preview before completing the assignment. You may wish to use students' alphabet book pages to create a classroom alphabet book. Ask for volunteers to complete pages for any missing letters.

Animal Adjectives (page 9): Gather and display pictures of a variety of animals—domestic, wild, zoo, farm, etc. After students complete the journal activity, let them share their descriptions while the rest of the class tries to guess the names of the animals being described.

Poetic Recipes (page 10): Offer students examples of real recipes to read. You may wish to discuss with the group the different parts and format of a recipe.

Happy Birthday! (page 11): Have several books about birthdays available in the classroom, like those suggested on the journal page. Talk with students, either before or after the activity, about their favorite birthday traditions.

Expressions (page 12): After completing the journal activity, have students predict what will happen next to the people in their pictures. Then, let each student write a story based on the picture and his or her predictions.

Interview with a Friend (page 13): Provide books about friends, including those listed on the journal page. Pair students and have them interview each other using the questions from their journals. If time allows, ask students to introduce their partners to the class with the information from their interviews.

Keys to Writing (page 14): Gather a collection of old keys to bring to class for this activity. Local antique shops often have old keys that can be purchased inexpensively. Or, ask parents to donate old keys. Have each student use his or her journal entry to write a short story or poem about the key.

Seasonal Sentences (page 15): Offer a selection of books about the seasons, like those listed on the journal page.

Teddy Bear Adventures (page 16): Provide books about teddy bears, including those listed on the journal page. Have students develop their short stories during writing time. Have them work with partners to edit and add to their stories. Then, allow each student to illustrate and publish his or her teddy bear adventure.

Wordless Picture Book (page 17): Share a selection of picture books with students, like those suggested on the journal page. Arrange a time for students to share their picture book stories with students in a kindergarten class.

Button, Button (page 18): Prepare a resealable, plastic bag with about 30 assorted buttons for each student.

Shapes All Around (page 19): Provide a selection of books about shapes, like those listed on the journal page. You may wish to take students on a walk around the school and let them add more observations to their shape lists.

Measuring Problem (page 20): Provide concrete objects for students to experiment with, such as a basketball, a yardstick, paper, string, interlocking cubes, stickers, etc.

One Half of a Whole (page 21): Gather several books about fractions and sharing, such as those listed on the journal page. After completing the journal activity, allow students to work in small groups to write and perform skits to show how to divide and share equally.

Animals from Space (page 22): Share books about shapes, like those listed on the journal page, with the class. Let students write stories about their space adventures and encounters with the shape creatures.

Math Vocabulary (page 23): Provide books about pond life. See the book list on the journal page for suggestions. You may wish to give students an example sentence, such as, "There are four more fish than turtles in the pond." Challenge students to write equations for their pond pictures, too.

Math in Action (page 24): Provide an assortment of old magazines. After completing the journal activity, post the math pictures on a bulletin board and allow students to read their math conversations to the class without telling which pictures were theirs. Let the class guess which pictures go with which conversations.

Roadside Stand (page 25): Let students write short stories about each of their three customers.

Tips and Extensions

Number Poems (page 26): Have volunteers read their poems to the class. Challenge the class to write equations to match the poems as they are read. Have students check their math at the end of each poem.

Saving for Goldfish (page 27): After completing the journal activity, encourage students to write stories about Kyle. Did he make enough money? How did he make the money? Did he take the special offer? What did he name the fish?

Flowers (page 28): Gather books about flowers, like those listed on the journal page, for the classroom. Let each student write a story about a day in the life of a flower growing in a garden. Allow time for illustrating and sharing.

Sounds Around (page 29): Share books about sound, such as those listed on the journal page. To help students add to their sound lists, you may wish to take students on a walk around the school grounds.

Pet Particulars (page 30): Offer a selection of books about pets, including those listed on the journal page. Have students write poems about favorite pets or animals and illustrate their poems.

Sight, Smell, and Touch (page 31): Bring in a variety of fruits and vegetables. You may wish to ask parents for donations. Cut open some fruits and vegetables to help students better experience them. If you have time and parent volunteers to help supervise, you can add taste to the list of qualities students observe. Be sure to check for student food allergies before choosing which fruits and vegetables to use for the activity.

Living and Nonliving (page 32): Let students write stories about nonliving things coming to life.

Animal Features (page 33): Provide a variety of books about animals and animal features. See the book list on the journal page for suggestions.

Balanced Meal (page 34): Supply students with old magazines. Let students describe their favorite meals.

Weather Watch (page 35): Share books about weather, including those listed on the journal page. After completing the activity, have students write scripts for weather reports based on their weather observations.

Weather Poems (page 36): Read aloud several poems about the weather. See the literature suggestions on the journal page. Let students illustrate their poems and allow volunteers to share their poems.

Mystery Box (page 37): After completing the journal activity, have each student choose an object and have him or her write a description of it without describing what it looks like. Descriptions can include how it feels, sounds, smells, etc.

Community Helpers (page 38): Gather books about community helpers, like those listed on the journal page, for the classroom. To introduce this activity, you may wish to invite one or more community helpers to visit the class.

What Do You Want? (page 39): Allow volunteers to share their writing.

Farm Life and City Life (page 40): Provide books about farm life and city life, like those listed on the journal page. Have each student to write and illustrate a short story about a child his or her age living either on a farm or in a city.

Map It! (page 41): Encourage students write about times when they or family members used maps.

Where Am I? (page 42): Suggest that each student write a letter to an alien, include his or her galactic address.

Travel through Time (page 43): Let students work in pairs to write skits about people traveling in different ways.

Folktales (page 44): Share several folktales with students, such as those listed on the journal page. Encourage students to write their own folktales. They may wish to include their own family customs and traditions.

Jobs in Your School (page 45): Let students share their stories with partners.

School Rules (page 46): Challenge each student to rewrite a school rule in the form of a poem.

Time to Celebrate! (page 47): Share books about holidays with students. See the book list on the journal page for suggestions.

Alphabet Books

Look at some alphabet books like those listed below. How do the different books show each letter? Are there pictures of things that start with the letter? Are there any words? Below, create a page from an alphabet book. Choose your favorite letter and write words and draw pictures to go with the letter. If you have time, try another letter on the back of this page.

Arf! Beg! Catch!: Dogs from A to Z by Henry Horenstein (Cartwheel Books, 1999)

A Gardener's Alphabet by Mary Azarian (Houghton Mifflin, 2000)

Appaloosa Zebra: A Horse Lover's Alphabet by Jessie Haas (Greenwillow Books, 2002)

Animalia by Graeme Base (Abrams Books for Young Readers, 1987)

Animal Adjectives

Animals aren't just cute or neat—they're fuzzy, prickly, and scaly! Find a picture of an animal that is displayed in your classroom, or in a book or magazine. Then, write a description of the animal using specific words that tell the details of the animal's mouth, legs, skin or fur, eyes, feet, tail, and more! Don't worry about spelling right now—just be descriptive!

Poetic Recipes

Read the poem below. It is written like a recipe. A recipe tells you what and how much to mix together to make something special. Use what you know about recipes and a special topic to write a recipe poem. You may wish to write a recipe for a happy party, a lazy Saturday, or a winning soccer game.

Recipe for a Happy Day!
Take two good friends
And mix till they start to giggle.
Add a funny joke,
And a pinch of a tickle.
Sprinkle in a secret or two,
And bake at 400 degrees
Until it laughs at you!

Happy Birthday!

Think about some of your past birthdays. What is your favorite birthday memory? What made it so good? Write about one thing that would make your next birthday the best birthday ever. Why would this thing make your birthday so special? Draw a picture to go with your writing. You may want to read some books about birthdays to help you with ideas. See the book list below.

Happy Birthday Biscuit! by Alyssa Satin Capucilli (HarperCollins, 1999)

Happy Birthday, Dear Amy by Marilyn Kaye (Skylark, 2001)

Happy Birthday, Lulu! by Caroline Uff (Walker & Co., 2000)

Expressions

Look through books and magazines to find a picture of someone whose face shows a strong emotion. Try to imagine why the person looks the way he or she does. Is the person sad? Happy? Surprised? Afraid? Why? In the space below, draw a picture of the person's face, describe the person's expression, and write what you think happened to make him or her feel that way.

Interview with a Friend

One way to meet new friends is to talk to new people and ask them questions about themselves. Do they have any hobbies? What are their favorite foods? Do they have any brothers or sisters? Make a list of questions you would like to ask a new friend. Try to list at least ten questions. Read books on friendship, like those listed below, for inspiration.

Buster's New Friend by Marc Brown and Stephen Krensky (Little Brown & Co., 2000)

Wanted: Best Friend by A. M. Monson (Dial Books, 1997)

Will You Be My Friend? by Nancy Tafuri (Scholastic, 2000)

Keys to Writing

Look through a collection of keys and choose one that you like best. Trace the outline of your key at the top of this page. Use your imagination to come up with a list of things that the key could unlock and write it below your tracing. Next, create a list of what someone might find when he or she uses the key. Finally, make a list of who the key might belong to.

My Key

I have an old key
That's important to me.
Hidden under my bed is a treasure box
That only my special key unlocks.
What's inside?
 Wouldn't you like to know?
 But I won't tell. Oh no, no, no.

Seasonal Sentences

Each season is different and different things are happening. Choose your favorite season and write sentences about the season using -ing words. For example, "Leaves are falling" or "Flowers are blooming." Think of as many -ing sentences as you can for your season, then draw a picture for your favorite. Read a seasonal book, like those listed below, to help you get started.

The Seasons of Arnold's Apple Tree by Gail Gibbons (Voyager Books, 1988)

Park Beat: Rhymin' Through the Seasons by Jonathan London (HarperCollins, 2001)

Here Comes Spring, and Summer, and Fall and Winter by Mary Murphy (Dorling Kindersley, 1999)

Jazz Up Your Journal Writing • CD-8066

Teddy Bear Adventures

Imagine your favorite teddy bear or other stuffed animal has gone on an exciting adventure! Write a short story telling about your bear's adventure. On the back of this page, draw a picture to go with your story. You might want to read a few stories about teddy bears to give you some ideas. Choose a story from the list below or pick another teddy bear story to read.

Corduroy Goes to School by Barbara G. Hennessy (Viking, 2002)

The Teddy Bear by David McPhail (Henry Holt & Co., 2002)

Willow on the River by Camilla Ashforth (Candlewick Press, 2002)

Wordless Picture Book

Look at several books that tell stories with just pictures and no words. (See the list below.) How do you tell the story to yourself as you "read" it? Choose a wordless picture book you like and write a story to go along with the pictures. Label your story with the page numbers from the book. Do you think your story would be the same as someone else's story for the same book? Why or why not?

The Hunter and the Animals by Tomie dePaola (Holiday House, 1988)

Time Flies by Eric Rohmann (Crown, 1994)

The Great Cat Chase by Mercer Mayer (McGraw-Hill, 2003)

Magpie Magic by April Wilson (Dial Books for Young Readers, 1999)

Button, Button

Take a bag of buttons and empty it onto your desk. First, count the buttons and write the total. Then, sort the buttons by color. Record the number of buttons in each group. Next, sort the buttons in a different way, maybe by size, and record the results. See how many different ways you can sort the buttons and keep track of the results below. Use the back of the page if you need more room.

The Little Rooster and the Diamond Button by Celia B. Lottridge (Groundwood Books, 2001)

Brass Button by Crescent Dragonwagon (Atheneum, 1997)

Grandma's Button Box by Linda Williams Abner (Kane Press, 2002)

Shapes All Around

Look at some books about shapes like those listed below. Then, look around the room and notice the shapes around you. Draw a line dividing the page and draw a big square in the top half and a big triangle in the bottom half. Divide the back of the page and draw a circle at the top and a rectangle at the bottom. In each shape, draw or write the names of things that are that shape.

Shapes by Robert Crowther (Candlewick Press, 2002)

Shape Spotters by Megan E. Bryant (Grosset & Dunlap, 2002)

A Star in My Orange: Looking for Nature's Shapes by Dana Meachen Rau (Millbrook Press, 2002)

Jazz Up Your Journal Writing • CD-8066

Measuring Problem

Imagine that you are an inspector at a sports ball factory. Your job is to make sure that all of the basketballs are the same size around. It's your first day on the job and you have all of these basketballs to measure, but only a yardstick to measure with. The yardstick is stiff and won't wrap around the basketballs. What can you do to make sure that all of the balls are measured correctly?

One Half of a Whole

Draw a circle and divide it equally in half. Is there another way to equally divide the circle in half? Draw it. Have you ever had to divide something in half to share with someone else? Write about that time or make up a story about dividing something in half to share with someone. You may want to read one of the stories listed below about dividing things into equal parts.

Rabbit and Hare Divide an Apple by Harriet Ziefert (Puffin, 1998)

Give Me Half! by Stuart J. Murphy (Scott Foresman, 1996)

The Hershey's® Milk Chocolate Bar Fractions Book by Jerry Pallotta (Cartwheel Books, 1999)

Animals from Space

Imagine that you are exploring in space and visit a strange planet where you discover animals that are made up completely of circles, triangles, rectangles, and squares! Write in your science log, describing in detail the animals you saw. What shapes make up their body parts? Do they have horns, three heads, or ten legs? Name your shape animals and draw their pictures.

Captain Invincible and the Space Shapes by Stuart J. Murphy (HarperTrophy, 2001)

The Wing on a Flea: A Book about Shapes by Ed Emberley (Little Brown & Co., 2001)

A Triangle for Adaora: An African Book of Shapes by Ifeoma Onyefulu (Dutton, 2000)

Math Vocabulary

Draw a large pond. Draw a big lily pad in the middle. Draw three frogs on the lily pad. Draw a rock in the upper right corner. Draw three turtles on the rock. Draw seven fish in the upper left corner of the pond. Draw a snake on the ground next to the lower left corner of the pond. Now, write five math sentences describing the pond. Use number words and words like equal, more, and less.

Pond Animals by Francine Galko (Heinemann Library, 2002)

A Pond in the Meadow by Sally Morgan (Thameside Press, 2000)

Turtle Splash! Countdown at the Pond by Cathryn Falwell (Greenwillow Books, 2001)

Math in Action

Look through old magazines to find a picture of math happening. It may be a person buying something or measuring something. Describe the scene and then write how math is being used. What might the people be saying? Write a mathematical conversation to go with the picture. If you have time, write about a situation when you used math that wasn't schoolwork.

Roadside Stand

Imagine that a nearby farm is full of ripe vegetables, and the farmer has asked you to sell his vegetables at a roadside stand. First, draw a catchy sign to advertise the vegetables. On the sign, draw each vegetable and write its selling price. Then, on the back of the page, create three customers and a list of the items they bought. Find the total that each customer should pay for his or her vegetables.

Number Poems

Read some funny poems like those in *Get Out of the Alphabet, Number 2!: Wacky Wednesday Puzzle Poems* by Kalli Dakos (Simon & Schuster Books for Young Readers, 1997). Then, write your own funny poem about numbers. Read the poem below for an example of a poem that uses numbers. If you have time, draw a picture to go with your poem.

Number Poem

Once, my family was mother, father, and me.
Altogether, we made three.
Along came baby brother to add one more,
And now our family is four.
When Uncle Bob and Aunt Kate
Bring the twins to visit, there are eight!
And when Gran and Granddad drop in, then
Our whole family adds up to ten!

Saving for Goldfish

Have you ever saved money to buy something special? Kyle is a boy who wants to save money to buy two goldfish, a box of fish food, and a large fishbowl. Look at the special offer and the price for each item listed below. Should Kyle take the special offer or buy each item individually? Why? Use math to support your answer. On the back of the page, write a list of ways Kyle could make and save money.

1 goldfish = $1.00
fish food = $2.00 a box
fishbowl = $3.00 for a small bowl
$5.00 for a large bowl
Special Offer: 2 goldfish, 2 boxes of fish food, and a large fish bowl for $10.00

Flowers

Look through pictures of flowers in old gardening magazines and flower catalogs to find a picture of a flower that you like. Cut out the flower and paste it on the center of the page. Then, label the parts: flower, stem, leaves, bud, and roots. If your picture doesn't show all of these parts, draw and label the missing ones. Then, write a description of the flower, including its size, color, and shapes of leaves and petals.

Growing Flowers by Tracy Nelson Maurer (Rourke Book Co., 2001)

Wildflowers around the Year by Hope Ryden (Clarion Books, 2001)

Flowers and Friends by Anita Holmes (Marshall Cavendish, 2000)

Jazz Up Your Journal Writing • CD-8066

Sounds Around

There are different sounds all around us even though we may not notice them all of the time. Make three lists: Sounds of Nature, Sounds of People, and Sounds of Machines. Then, close your eyes and notice the sounds around you. Write words for the sounds you heard under the correct headings. Then, think of other sounds that would belong under each heading and add them to your lists.

Read books about sounds!

What's That Noise? by Michelle Edwards and Phyllis Root (Candlewick Press, 2002)

Hearing Things by Allan Fowler (Bt Bound, 2001)

A Rumpus of Rhymes: A Book of Noisy Poems by Bobbi Katz (Dutton Children's Books, 2001)

Jazz Up Your Journal Writing • CD-8066

Pet Particulars

Have you ever had to take care of a pet? What did it eat? What other care did it need? Have you ever observed an animal's behavior? How did it act in different situations? Write an article for a science journal describing a pet or other animal. Tell about where it lives, what it eats, what it does during the day and night, and any other facts about it. Draw a picture of the pet to go with your article.

That's My Dog! by Rick Walton (Penguin Group, 2001)

Henry and Mudge and Annie's Perfect Pet by Cynthia Rylant (Simon & Schuster Books for Young Readers, 2001)

How to Talk to Your Cat by Jean Craighead George (HarperCollins, 2000)

Sight, Smell, and Touch

Choose a fruit or vegetable to observe with three of your senses—sight, smell, and touch. Carefully observe the fruit or vegetable and draw it on the page. Then, describe exactly how it looks, feels, and smells. Use specific words like rough or fuzzy instead of words like weird or good. If you have time, choose another fruit or vegetable to describe and compare the two.

Touching by Sharon Gordon (Scholastic, 2002)

Smelling by Sharon Gordon (Scholastic, 2002)

Seeing by Alvin Silverstein (Millbrook Press, 2001)

Jazz Up Your Journal Writing • CD-8066

Living and Nonliving

Divide the page into two halves. In the top half, draw a picture of something that is living. In the bottom half, draw a picture of something that is nonliving. Then, write three to five facts about the living thing that tell you that it is living. Then, write facts about the nonliving thing that tell you that it is not living. If you have time, write lists of living and nonliving things on the back of the page.

Animal Features

Look at several books about animals. (See the list below.) Notice features of each animal that are different, such as a trunk, a long tail, big ears, a long neck, etc. Do these features help the animal do something specific? Choose an animal that you like and write about what makes this animal special and different from other animals. Draw a picture of the animal. Then, write a story about the animal using its special features.

Tails by Elizabeth Miles (Heinemann Library, 2002)

Feathers and Tails: Animal Fables from around the World by David Kherdian (Philomel Books, 1992)

Beaks by Sneed B. Collard (Charlesbridge Pub., 2002)

Balanced Meal

We should always try to eat some food from each food group at each meal. We can eat more foods from some food groups than from other groups. Draw a circle below for a plate. Then, either paste pictures of food cut from magazines or draw pictures on the plate to show a balanced meal. Pay attention to how big your servings are. Which food groups have the biggest serving sizes? The smallest?

What Food Is This?
by Rosemarie Hausherr
(Bt Bound, 1999)

*Staying Healthy:
Eating Right*
by Alice B. McGinty
(Franklin Watts, 1999)

Weather Watch

It's hard to not notice the weather each day. What kinds of weather are there? Draw a symbol for each type of weather you can think of and label each. Then, for two weeks, write the date and draw one symbol to show what the weather is like that day. At the end of the two weeks, answer these questions: How many days of each type of weather were there? Was the weather normal for the time of year? Why or why not?

Rain and Shine
by Deborah Kespert
(Two-Can, 2000)

Twister! by Bill Haduch
(Dutton Books, 1999)

DK Guide to Weather by Michael Allaby
(DK Publishing, 2000)

Jazz Up Your Journal Writing ◆ CD-8066

35

Weather Poems

What do you do in different types of weather? How do you feel in different types of weather? Complete each line to write a weather poem.

When it rains, I . . .
When it is sunny, I . . .
When it is really cold, I . . .
When it is windy, I . . .
When it is dark and cloudy, I . . .

Storm Coming!
Poems by
Audrey B. Baird
(Wordsong/Boyds
Mills Press, 2001)

Let's Count the Raindrops
illustrated by Fumi
Kosaka (Viking, 2001)

Mystery Box

Can you picture something in your mind just from how it feels? Try putting your hand inside a mystery box and feeling the items inside. Can you guess what they are? Feel each item in the box and draw a picture of what you think it looks like. When you finish, open the mystery box and compare your drawing to the actual item. How good were your guesses?

Community Helpers

There are many people in a community that work to help others. Make a list of these jobs, such as a mail carrier and firefighter. Then, choose one community helper and write three sentences that tell how this person helps or serves others. You may want to read a book from the list below to give you more information. If you have time, draw a picture of your community helper.

Community Helpers from A to Z by Bobbie Kalman (Crabtree Publishing Company, 1997)

We Need Mail Carriers by Lola M. Schaefer (Pebble Books, 1999)

What Do You Want?

Have you ever made a list of things that you wanted for your birthday or for a holiday? You probably didn't get everything on your list, but it was okay because you didn't *need* them. What kinds of things do you need? Write a list of things you need and a list of things you want. Then, write about what would happen if you didn't get what you wanted and what would happen if you didn't get what you needed.

Jazz Up Your Journal Writing • CD-8066

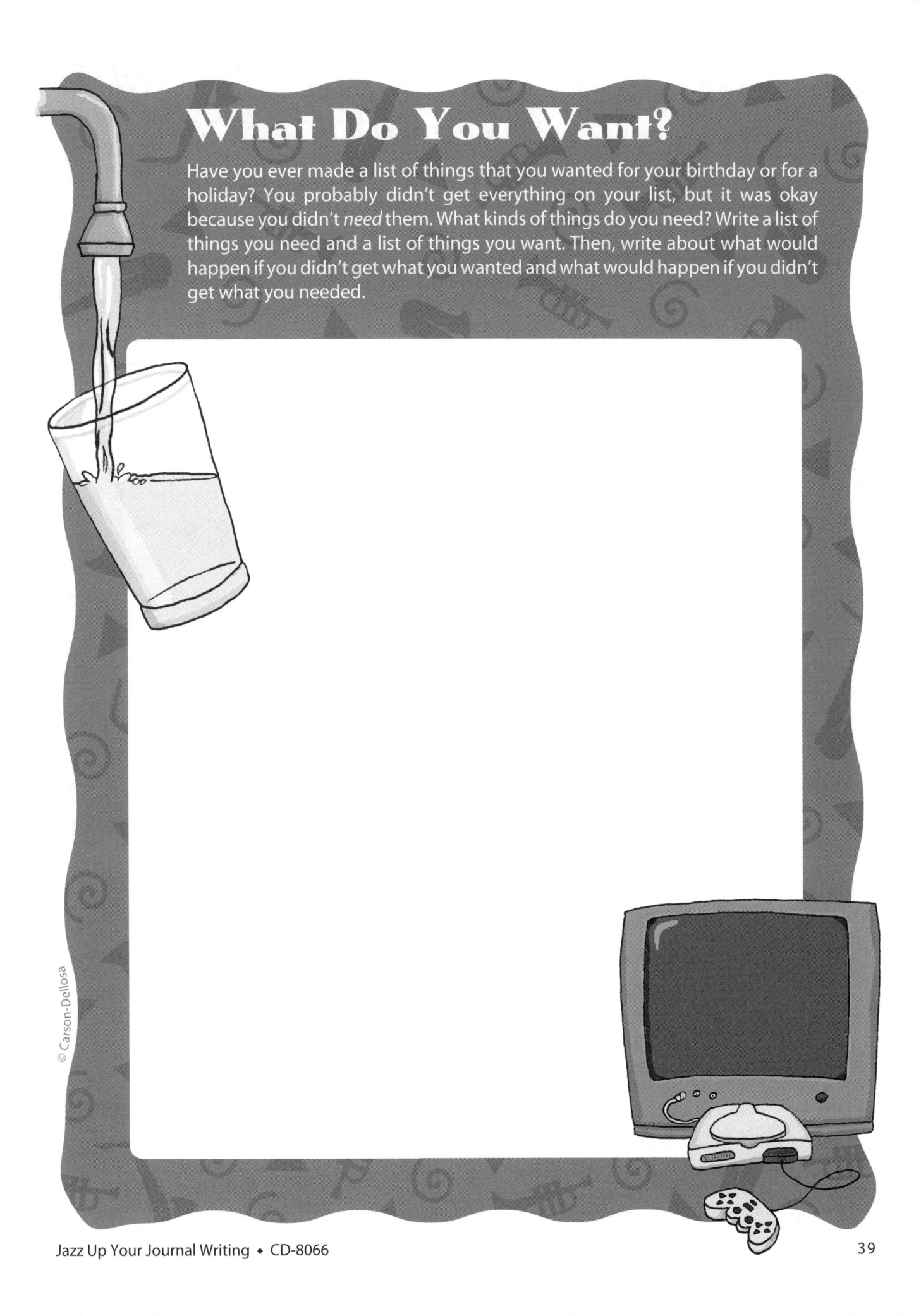

Farm Life and City Life

Think about what life is like on a farm and in a city. What kinds of things do people do in each place? Label three lists below: Farm, City, and Both. Then, write things that people do on a farm, in a city, and in both places. Read some of the books listed below to help you with ideas. Circle the things in your lists that you do where you live.

TOWN CENTER

From Dawn Till Dusk by Natalie Kinsey-Warnock (Houghton Mifflin, 2002)

Listen to the City by Rachel Isadora (Putnam, 2000)

Busy, Busy City Street by Cari Meister (Viking, 2000)

Jazz Up Your Journal Writing ♦ CD-8066

Map It!

Look at some different maps. Do the maps have symbols on them that stand for different things, like parks, hospitals, and airports? Is there a map key, or legend, that tells what each symbol means? Think of all of the things in your bedroom. Below, make a map key with symbols for each thing in your room. If you have time, draw a map of your room on the back of the page.

Jazz Up Your Journal Writing • CD-8066

Where Am I?

Do you know what your address is? Do you know what your galactic address is? Pretend that you must give your address to an alien that lives in another galaxy. Below, write your galactic address. Start with the name of our galaxy, then name the solar system of the sun. Continue with your planet, continent, country, state or province, county, city or town, and finally your street address.

Travel through Time

How many different ways have you traveled? By boat? By car? Walking? Label three lists below: Long Ago, Today, and Future. Then, write the ways people traveled in old times, ways people travel today, and ways you think people will travel in the future. Some ways to travel, like walking, might be in all three lists. On the back of the page, draw your favorite way to travel.

Jazz Up Your Journal Writing • CD-8066

Folktales

One way to learn about the customs of families and cultures around the world is to read folktales. Read folktales from the books listed below and choose one that you like. Draw a line across the middle of the page and write "alike" in the top half and "different" in the bottom half. Then, write two or three sentences that tell how the family or people in the folktale are alike and different from your family and friends.

Tuck-Me-In Tales: Bedtime Stories from Around the World by Margaret Read MacDonald (August House, 2001)

Little Folk: Stories from Around the World by Paul Robert Walker (Harcourt Brace, 1997)

Jobs in Your School

A school is like a small community. Each person in a school has an important job with certain responsibilities. Your job is to be a student. List the responsibilities of a student. What are some other jobs in your school? Choose a job in your school and write a story about what might happen if all of the people with that job stopped coming to work.

School Rules

Think about the rules you follow in school. Do you think the rules work well? Are there things that have been left out of the rules that you think should be added? What problems are there in your school that a rule could help solve? Think of five rules for your school that you think are important. Write the rules in a positive way. For example, instead of "Don't shout in the cafeteria," say "Use quiet voices in the cafeteria."

Time to Celebrate!

What holidays do you and your family celebrate? Do you have special traditions for each holiday? Write a paragraph about your favorite holiday and write about how your family celebrates. Draw a picture to go with your paragraph. Do you think other people celebrate this holiday the same way you do? Read some of the books about different holiday traditions listed below.

Moonbeams, Dumplings & Dragon Boats by Nina Simonds, Leslie Swartz, and The Children's Museum, Boston (Harcourt, 2002)

The Fiestas by George Ancona (Benchmark Books, 2001)

Rosh Hashanah and Yom Kippur by David F. Marx (Children's Press, 2001)